A Book About My Parents

A Child's Creation

Randi Lynn Millward

Instructions:
This book is a children's activity book. The sentences are started but left incomplete for the child to finish in his or her own words. The adjacent pages are intentionally blank so that the child may create his or her own illustrations.
The artist may draw with crayons or colored pencils, tape pictures to the pages, use stickers, or us any other parent-approved age-appropriate artistic medium that doesn't seep through the paper.

Disclaimer: Author/Publisher not responsible for any loss or damage to anyone or anything caused by or related to use of this book or any medium used in or on this book. Parents bear the sole responsibility for their children's safety.

ISBN 10: 1-943771-10-3
ISBN 13: 978-1-943771-10-3

All content is copyright 2019 by Millward Creative and Randi Lynn Millward.
All rights reserved.
No part of this book may be copied, transmitted, sold, translated, photocopied, or otherwise reproduced by any means without written permission from the author/publisher.
Cover photo is property of Randi Lynn Millward and Millward Creative and may not be copied, transmitted, sold, translated, photocopied, or otherwise reproduced by any means without written permission from the author/publisher/illustrator.
More books by this author may be found at www.Amazon.com and other participating retailers.

A Book About My Parents

by

____

Age: ______________

Date: ____________

My parents are

____

____

____

____

____

____

_____________________.

My parents

____

____

____

____

____

____

____

____

______________________________.

My parents like to

____

____

____

____

____

____

____

____________________.

My parents don't like

____

____

____

____

____

____

____

______________________.

My parents are really good at

____

____

____

____

____

____

_____________________.

I like when my parents

____

____

____

____

____

____

____

______________________.

My parents like when I

____

____

____

____

____

____

____

____________________.

My favorite thing to do with my parents is

____

____

____

____

____

___________________.

I have fun when my parents and I

____

____

____

____

____

____

___________________.

My parents say

____

____

____

____

____

____

____

____

______________________.

I like to show my parents

____

____

____

____

____

____

____

______________________.

My parents laugh when

____

____

____

____

____

____

____

_______________________.

Something special about my parents is

____

____

____

____

____

____

_______________________.

Sometimes my parents

____

____

____

____

____

____

____

___________________.

My favorite thing about my parents is

____

____

____

____

____

____

_______________________.

I hope that someday my parents

____

____

____

____

____

____

__________________.

I love my parents because

____

____

____

____

____

____

___________________.

www.ingramcontent.com/pod-product-compliance
Lightning Source LLC
LaVergne TN
LVHW010108110826
845155LV00028B/549

9781943771103